STOP BULLYING!

TREAT OTHERS THE WAY YOU WANT TO BE TREATED

For Elementary, Middle and High Schools

BEVERLY JEAN PARAMORE

2nd Revised Edition

Printed in the United States of America

ISBN: 978-0-578-62678-9

Beverly Paramore, Publisher
Chicago, IL

www.preventschoolbullying@gmail.com

TABLE OF CONTENTS

Dedicated to Students

INgTRODUCTION

The subject of this book is about school bullying. Also, information in this book is a tool to help you understand not only what school bullying is, but what school bullying looks like. The goal of this book is to help counteract school bullying. The following explanation is a verbal snapshot of what school bullying looks like.

School bullying behavior sometimes takes place out of the sight of others. Bullying can be a subtle behavior. An example of subtle behavior is someone said mean things to you and you told them this hurts your feelings. The one who is bullying might reply, "I'm just joking." Or, the one who physically bullies in front of others is saying non-verbally, "I don't care who sees me commit this violent behavior towards you." Or, it could be on the world stage which is social media (cyberbullying).

No matter what grade level the bullying attack occurs in or how it occurs, no matter how subtle it is school bullying is bullying.

There is nothing positive about school bullying because there is no such thing as friendly bullying or "I'm just joking" bullying. If you bully, you are totally bullying on purpose – to hurt and tear down self-worth of the student you are bullying.

School bullying is a cruel repetitive behavior that ultimately attacks and tears down another student's well-being.

A school bully is someone who targets or looks for a victim who can be easily frightened. Bullies pick on students who they think are weaker than they are or who is actually smaller in body size than they are or who is younger than they are. Sometimes bullies will even target students who they think are smarter than they are.

Bullying is an act of frightening someone (which is called intimidation). The word frighten means make someone scared, afraid or terrified. Some students become so terrified and hopeless that they commit suicide as a result of being bullied. Sometimes school bullying occurs because the one who bullies might be getting bullied in other areas in their life. It's called "The Bullying Cycle."

In some cases the student who bullies has low self-esteem. What can be done about that? Let's build up everybody's self-esteem.

Instead of concentrating on tearing somebody's self-worth down, why not build up somebody's self-worth starting with you. Do you know why? Because you have potential and you are valuable human being.

Everybody has potential. I believe if you apply yourselves and learn about the potential inside of you, you will begin to believe in yourself. You know yourself better than anybody. Make a positive difference in your own life. There are youth at various ages who have invented things to make the world a better place to live in. Search for teen inventors.

A 13 year old invented a Braille printer (for those who have vision impairment or vision loss) using a Lego set as a proto type. His name is Shubham Banerjee. This printer is affordable for people to purchase. Before his printer, Braille printers were so expensive that people with visual impairment or visual loss couldn't afford them. His printer has made a difference for people around the world. At this writing, he is now 18 years old.

Intel eventually heard about it and invested in his Braille printer where it became a printer that could be sold to consumers. When Shubham was 17 years old, Yahoo bought his company for $30 million.

You might be saying to yourself, you don't have the money. Shubham didn't either. That's why the first one he made was made out of Legos.

In 2013, a 13 year-old girl invented something for pets and their owners. I am not going to tell you what it is – Google it. Her name is Brooke Martin and her dog's name is Kayla.

There are corporations who support education and gives out grants and scholarships. You could go to college to earn a college degree and perhaps put your ideas out there. You just never know unless you try.

After reading this book, your understanding will be broadened. You will be encouraged to take the challenge to become a role model of positive change. You can start today, by becoming the best you can be.

The ultimate goal of this book is for everybody to value themselves. You are valuable and you have potential.

You are a very valuable human being and the world, whether it's in your neighborhood or across the globe, is waiting for you and for your contribution to society.

It is already in you, you just have to discover what it is.

LEARNING HOW TO LEARN

The definition of the word learn is by experience, studying or by being taught.

It is very important to learn how to make good decisions in order to get the best results. Do we make the right decisions all the time? No. Everybody experiences this from time to time. However, we still learn things when we don't make the right decisions. We have the opportunity to learn how to get it right the next time. Some people call this learning from our mistakes.

Making good decisions regarding school may require you to seek advice from your parents and/or from your teachers.

For example, you may be having difficulty understanding a subject in school.

You can make one of two decisions to solve this problem.

One choice is you are too embarrassed to tell your parents or teachers you don't understand the subject. Because you are too embarrassed to let someone know, you don't seek help and fail the subject.

You might be thinking you don't want to ask because people might laugh. Parents and teachers won't laugh. Some students might. So what! They are not going to grow up to be you. You are responsible for your own learning and gaining of knowledge. When you ask for help, you earn respect.

You got to do what you got to do (in a positive and honest way) for your future. You are responsible for your own learning. You have to learn to make good decisions and one good decision is to learn how to study and to ask for help if you need help.

An example of good study habits is read your lesson to study for your test (not necessarily the night before you take your test). Set aside time to study. This way you will find out what you are having trouble with, if anything, and study that topic a little bit more. For example spelling; practice spelling the words verbally or written. If you write the word down, go back to see if you spelled it correctly. If you don't know the meaning of some words, look up look up the meaning. It will really give you more understanding into what you are reading. Google subjects online to get more information about topics you are studying.

Admitting that you need help in school is not being weak, but just the opposite; it is a sign of strength. Guess what? The reason you are in school is to learn. Part of the learning process is to ask questions to get answers in order to gain understanding of what the subject is about.

So, the second choice you have is you can tell your parents and/or teachers (if in high school you can tell your school counselor) that you don't understand a subject. Get help, gain the understanding and get good grades.

Make up your mind you are going to study and make the right decision to learn. You might surprise yourself because you just might learn you enjoy studying and learning.

LET'S BE REAL

You desire to have best friends in school. Number one thing to know, however, is if another student is treating you mean on a consistent basis, that is not a friend.

Because of fear of losing friends or being rejected by your peers, some of you might accept being treated mean. Being treated mean is a form of being bullied. It makes you doubt being accepted, it hurts your feelings and tears down self-esteem. Even though you are being treated mean, you may still think that these students are your friends.

Here's an example. The evening before everybody met over a friend's house and the next day they talked about how much fun they had in front of you. You feel left out. You might say something like this, 'Oh, I didn't know you all were meeting up.' They might answer, 'Oh, it was a last minute thing. Did you want to come?' That's hurtful. Of course you wanted to be included.

Now your feelings are hurt. Why are your feelings hurt? Because you don't feel valued, not accepted or good enough to be genuinely a part of that group. If this happens more than once, you begin to feel like an outcast or rejected. What do you do?

Stop hanging around with that group. Learn how to observe situations. If it happens more than once, let's say twice then they are sending you a message. You might cry because you really wanted to be friends with them. You must realize those are not your friends, you are not valued in that group. That doesn't mean, however, that you are not a valuable person. You are just not valuable to them. You are valuable. You have to realize you are not valuable with that group. You are valuable (no matter what they think about you) and you are valuable without that group. They are not the end all of friends.

Become an observer and see who seems to be a person like you and see if that is someone who can be a friend. You all click and have a nice time without pressure of trying to fit in.

Here is another example. There may be a student you enjoy being around. One of the things you really like about this person is that he or she is funny and makes you laugh. This student has the ability to make others laugh and feel happy. Who wouldn't want to be around a person like that? You're having a bad day. You tell your friend and she says something funny – now you're laughing and feeling better already.

Initially, when you were getting acquainted with this student, you probably weren't' used to observing behavior in others.

If this is a fun person to be around, you just saw that one side of that student.

However, in the initial stages of getting to know this student, you should observe the characteristics of this person. How do they act and how does he or she treat other people.

The purpose of observing is if this is someone you would like to be friends with or just hang around with you need to learn this person. By observing this person, you will learn about this person's good and/or, maybe, not so good behavior.

Even though this student is fun to be around and may make you laugh, if this person has a habit of talking negatively about other students – like putting them down in front of other students, then you are learning the not so good behavior about this student. If you are comfortable with this behavior then that is one thing. But if you have a problem with it, then that is another thing.

When you learn that this student talks about other students negatively and may even make them cry, etc., do you still want to be friends with this student? Are you comfortable being with this person when he or she shows that aggressive behavior? Or, are you embarrassed being with this person?

Let's say that you are okay with this student's mean behavior towards other students. It might seem harmless to you, even fun. You might even tell that student 'you shouldn't do that, laughing while you are telling that person to stop.

I don't know if you realize this, but if you are with this student when the mean behavior is being displayed, other students will think that you are just like that student (a mean person or a bully); even if you really are not.

Sometimes students may choose you to be their friend. Stay in observation mode. They must be observed, too. You can determine if this is a student that you want to be friends with. You choose your friends.

If you notice a friend's behavior has changed towards you, and is saying mean things about you in front of other students or in private, this could be one of two things happening. Either this friend is just really teasing you or this person is really treating you mean on purpose. Parent's advice is helpful.

Now it's time to go into an observation mode to observe this new development of behavior in an established friendship.

When you tell your friend that your feelings are hurt when he or she says mean things to you, the reply could be, 'I'm just joking. You can't take a joke?' You might even be told that you are too sensitive.'

One of the ways you will be able to tell if this is a real friend is if the mean comments stop once you tell that person your thoughts about how it makes you feel. A real friend will not say that anymore. A friend, who stops because you are uncomfortable and your feelings are hurt, respects and values you enough to stop.

However, if this person continues to say mean things time after time after time; this is not a real friend. Also remember, bullying behavior is a cruel repetitive behavior. This student may be a bully.

Let's be real. There may be times people are not going to stop laughing at you or say mean things about you. This is why you have to believe in yourself and not believe negative words that others say about you. You know yourself better than they do. You can choose not to believe what they say about you.

If peers laugh at you, you could lighten things up and laugh too. By laughing when they laugh, puts you in control over this situation by defeating their purpose to make you feel bad.

One of the highest causes of depression in youth is caused by bullying and cyberbullying. As you know, cyberbullying is being bullied on social media.

If you are being bullied online, your parents should know. Bullying takes place on social media on a regular basis. You should inform your parents if you are being bullied online.

There is information in this book that will tell you and your parents what steps can be taken in this situation to alleviate cyberbullying.

Sadly, and as we have heard from time to time, some students have committed suicide as a result of verbal abuse, physical confrontations and cyberbullying by other students.

Having respect for life is a good reason to stop bullying students online or in any other form.

Another good reason to stop bullying online is because one day you are going to be seeking employment, but right now you are participating in cyberbullying. You are establishing your own historical track record of your bullying behavior on the world stage. Remember, the world stage is the internet.

Employers look for candidates who are trustworthy, who have integrity and who are team players. Potential employers sometimes search the internet to get a glimpse of who you are and what you've done. If a potential employer searches online for information about your past, and cyberbullying activity or any other negative information about you pops up, could determine if you get that job or not.

Consider this. Online bullying has a two-fold consequence. You may be so intent on destroying the reputation of another student or if you are taunting them to commit suicide (interpreted as 'kill yourself') at this time; you are destroying the reputation (or life) as well as destroying your reputation in the future. This information will be online for a very long time.

Before you participate in this type of behavior, stop to think about your future. This is the time now to think about the consequences of bullying behavior.

There are employers who will probably still hire you based on degrees earned, experience and accomplishments, but just know that school bullying online has taken information from the school yard, so to speak, to the world stage. Technology is advanced and is still advancing and will continue to advance even more. For example, someone from the Netherlands bullied a student here in the United States. They caught him.

WHO IS A BULLY?

The *Merriam-Webster Dictionary* defines a bully as one who is habitually cruel to others who are weaker than they are. Youth who bully usually do not bully students that are their own size and stronger than they are.

There are many reasons why youth bully. Some students who bully believes displaying anger represents strength and power.

It takes strength and power not to bully other students. It takes real strength and power to control yourself. It's called self-control.

INTROSPECTIVE MIRROR

Introspective means the act or process of looking inwardly at oneself. How do you do that? By listening to your thoughts. This chapter is about thought. Thought is the process of thinking.

A conscious thought is something you're engaged with (in the moment). You are paying attention and are aware of what you're saying to yourself in your mind. You know why you are thinking the thought. You're not saying to yourself, 'I know why I am thinking this thought,' but you are engaged in conversation with yourself. Yes. It's true. We do talk to ourselves and we answer ourselves. The term for this thought process is called internal monologue. It's making a choice to choose a thought in the moment.

An internal monologue, also called self-talk or inner speech, is a person's inner voice which provides a running verbal monologue of thoughts while we are conscious. It is usually tied to a person's sense of self.

There is also internal monologue called chatter. Chatter speech is talking rapidly or incessantly – without interruption. So, there are different ways we talk to ourselves in thought.

Another way of talking to ourselves is called our imagination. This is the process of forming mental images or pictures in our minds. We can see images (pictures) in our minds of what we are thinking about.

We make decisions based on (1) emotions (our feelings), or (2) rationalizing (defining a reason for a course of action), or (3) intellect (with knowledge).

If we analyze or examine our thoughts and decide not to act in an adverse way; it could save us from getting into a whole lot of trouble. We always have the option of making good decisions or bad decision. This is why we should 'listen' to how we talk to ourselves.

Emotions are love, hate, anger, happy, sad, depression, jealousy, fear, etc. This is not the entire list of emotions, but a few.

I want to interject something here before going on. If you have a friend who talks about not wanting to live anymore, you should take that seriously. If you are being told this information, this is a cry for help. You should tell a trusted adult about this.

Let's explore the emotion of feeling jealous or jealousy. The word jealousy means resenting a person who is enjoying success or advantage. The word resent means being angry or annoyed in a way that makes you feel mad from a sense of insult. Insult means speak to or treat with disrespect or scornful abuse. Scorn means you feel no respect for the individual because you think that he or she is worthless. One would have to be very strong within herself or himself to admit that they have a jealousy issue. Do you have a jealousy issue? Do you feel these emotions?

A student could be jealous of another student because the other student is making better grades.

Youth who are considered smart and who are picked on are sometimes called nerds and geeks. These words are meant to be hurtful, but shouldn't be. The intent is meant to make a student feel bad about being smart.

If you are jealous of someone you think is smarter than you, there is a solution. The solution is for you to make better grades. You can do it. You don't have to be jealous. Remember you are in school to learn.

This goal is obtainable. You can get tutoring or join study groups. It is possible for you to make better grades.

To those who support bullying youth in school by being spectators and/or participants (by laughing, etc.), you need to ask yourself the following questions. Is this something you really enjoy doing? Do you feel guilty, but are just going along?

Does it make you sad when another student is bullied? Do you feel sorry for that student? If you are not happy even though you laugh, do you feel guilty if you are participating? If your answer is yes to any of these questions, then you are not being true to you. You may need to take the steps to make a positive change. If you participate in bullying on the outside and feeling sad on the inside, you are not at peace in your thoughts.

By making a decision to change your behavior, can make a positive difference in your own life and in the lives of other students. This is possible.

TECHNIQUES AND RESOURCES

The following teaches students and parents how to respond to bullying by phone or cyberbullying. If you take these steps, your parents should know or could assist you.

The following responses are distributed by the Illinois Attorney General's Office:

1) Tell your parents and/or trusted adult. If you are in school tell your teacher or school administrators. If you feel your life is in danger, call 911.[1]

2) Print all instances of cyberbullying to have a record of all instances.

---

[1] Please Note: Depending on your age, discuss with your parents under what circumstances calls to 911 should be made.

3) Preserve electronic evidence. If you receive a mean or threatening message do not delete the message. You should take a screenshot of a text message or store the message in a folder. There may be important electronic information that law enforcement can trace the source.

4) Report improper content and usage to the perpetrator's website or internet service provider (*e.g.*, Comcast or AT&T, etc.). Most websites and internet service, cell phone providers should have a terms or service agreement that prohibits members from using their service to harass or threaten others. Most websites and internet service providers also supply a link to report this type of abuse (check with your cell phone provider). If you

are too young to do these techniques, ask your parents to do so for you.

5) Ignore the sender. You do not have to respond. In fact, responding can escalate the situation.

6) Block the sender. If ignoring the person does not improve the situation, you can call your phone company,[2] to block the number so that individual can no longer call your phone. You can also remove a person from your buddy list.

This is the end of the information from the Illinois Attorney General's Office.

The following is information how to diminish school bullying or cyberbullying. This

---

[2] This is my suggestion, because what I am about to say is not on the respond list from the Illinois Attorney General's Office. You may not be the one authorized to speak to the phone company, so let your parent(s) or guardian know so they can have the sender blocked. (yr. 2011)

instruction is to keep your personal information or business personal.

Personal information is often spread on social networks to make students feel rejected and disrespected. Other students are encouraged to join in. The intent of online bullying is to destroy your reputation.

Comments made on social media are not true all the time. True information can be posted on social media if you have shared it with someone. Personal information that has been made public can be devastating.

A technique to use to determine if you should share personal information is ask yourself 'would I be embarrassed if anyone knew this information about me?' If the answer is yes, you definitely will not want to share that information. You don't want to take any chances.

You may not want to disclose information of prescribed medications; or of operations you have had, past or present to any of your friends. And the rest you can decide what it is that you will not discuss with friends. Remember a friendly relationship could change. If you are not sure, discuss with your parents what information is not appropriate to share with friends.

Personal information is just what it says it is - personal. You are not obligated to share it with your friends if you don't want to.

However, there is an exception to the rule. You know parents have a right to ask you questions, so I am not talking about parents.

Use this simple technique as a friendly response to not disclose your personal information. If you are asked something personal or something that is too embarrassing to share just say 'that's personal.' Everybody should understand that. If they continue asking, just say 'it's personal.'

However, you might think if you don't share your personal information, you will lose your friends. If the student asking you is a real friend, you will still be friends after you don't disclose your personal information.

If someone asks and they get mad when you tell them 'that's personal' is probably not a real friend. He or she is just seeking something to gossip about.

If someone becomes insistent and keeps asking, tell your parents. They can advise you.

You can always ask your parents for suggestions.

You know how students make fun of other students and they are laughing at you and others laugh with them? The following techniques could be for this group. You could (1) ignore them or (2) start laughing, too. More than likely, they are going to stop laughing, and start looking at you and might even ask you 'what are you laughing at?' You could answer, 'you were laughing and I joined in."

Two things could happen. If you laugh, it's going to take the fun out of them laughing at you (if they are being mean). They were looking for a different reaction from you. It ruined their making fun of you. Or, everybody is going to start cracking up laughing for real because they didn't expect that reaction either.

This is a judgement call for elementary and high school students. I would suggest you discuss ahead of time how to handle bullying situations with your parents. If the bullying event is handled right away by your teacher, or school administrator, still mention it to your parents. You can tell your parents that your teacher or school administrator handled it. Your parents will appreciate that.

However, if it resurfaces after the teacher has handled it or a new incident occurs, which could happen, let your parents know. Ask your parent to speak to your teacher.

The history or foundation of education in the United States is for formal and informal learning. You are not in school to bully and students are not in school to be bullied, but all go to school to learn and to get an education.

You are going to school to learn. School is for learning and learning can be fun.

S.E.A.

S.E.A. is an acronym I created to help you to remember these three words. They are as follows:

(1) **S**ympathy - feeling sorrow for another;

(2) **E**mpathy – feeling what the other person feels; putting yourself in that person's place; and

(3) **A**pathy – indifference; don't care if someone is suffering.

If you feel sympathy, you feel sorry for the student who is being bullied.

If you imagine what is being done to the student is being done to you and you can imagine what that student's pain and suffering feels like, that is empathy.

Apathy is an emotion of the student who is bullying. There is indifference of the bully of the student's pain and suffering who is being bullied.

We have to believe in ourselves even in cases when it seems that no one else believes in us. You may want to stop bullying other students. There is potential in you to do positive things with your life. It is possible.

Potential means capable of becoming. You have the potential in you to make a positive difference in your life and in the lives of others. We all have the potential to do incredible things with our lives.

Words are very powerful. Speak these words to yourself THERE IS POTENTIAL IN ME TO DO GREAT THINGS. Repeat these words to yourself from time to time.

When you first start saying these words to yourself, it is going to sound empty. But keep saying them to yourself and one day you will believe it.

Also, speak these words to yourself, I WILL TREAT OTHERS WITH THE RESPECT THE WAY I WANT TO BE TREATED.

You are your own best friend or you are your own worst enemy. Choose to be your own best friend.

ARE YOU WILLING?

These are questions you can ask yourself. If you are bullying other students what are you willing to do?

Are you willing to stop bullying other students?

Are you willing to admit to yourself that you have hurt other students emotionally or physically in school or online or told them to kill themselves?

Are you willing to feel empathy for those students you have bullied? In other words, how would you feel if someone bullied you in school?

Are you willing to feel sorry because you have bullied other students?

Are you willing to say to yourself you are sorry?

Are you willing to say you are sorry to the student(s) you bullied?

Saying you're sorry takes strength. In doing so, you will earn a whole lot of respect from others and mainly for yourself.

If you do these things, you will feel so good about your decision and you will feel really good about yourself. Others will respect you and, most of all, you will respect yourself. This could also save a life.

This is the first day of the rest of your life. You can do this!

CONCLUSION

You don't want to look back in life and regret wasting this precious time in your life. Decisions you make in your life now can affect your future.

On the following pages there is a challenge questionnaire.

Even though you may not bully other students, you may want to read over these questions anyway. Everyone can answer challenge question number 50.

Today really is the first day of the rest of your life. Your life is you. What are you going to do with you?

CHALLENGE QUESTIONNAIRE

CHALLENGE QUESTIONNAIRE

CHALLENGE QUESTIONNAIRE

When you answer these questions be honest with yourself and remember that these questions relates only to the school environment.

Even if you are not displaying bullying behavior, it may be interesting to read these questions.

These questions are intended to help you to realize what you may want to do differently to accomplish positive things in the future.

These questions are meant for you to answer and to be honest with yourself. You do not necessarily have to share your answers with anyone if you choose not to.

The answers you provide will help you to take an honest look at yourself and help you to recognize what you want to change about yourself. This is a self-evaluation.

1. What does school bullying mean?

2. Do I bully others in school??

3. Why?

CHALLENGE QUESTIONNAIRE

4. Are you jealous of this student?

5. (a) Why don't you like this student? (b) Is it possible you don't have a clear reason why you don't like this student? If you do have a reason, please write it down.

CHALLENGE QUESTIONNAIRE

6. Do you say mean things to other student?

7. Do you feel bad when you bully others?

8. Why do you feel bad about bullying others?

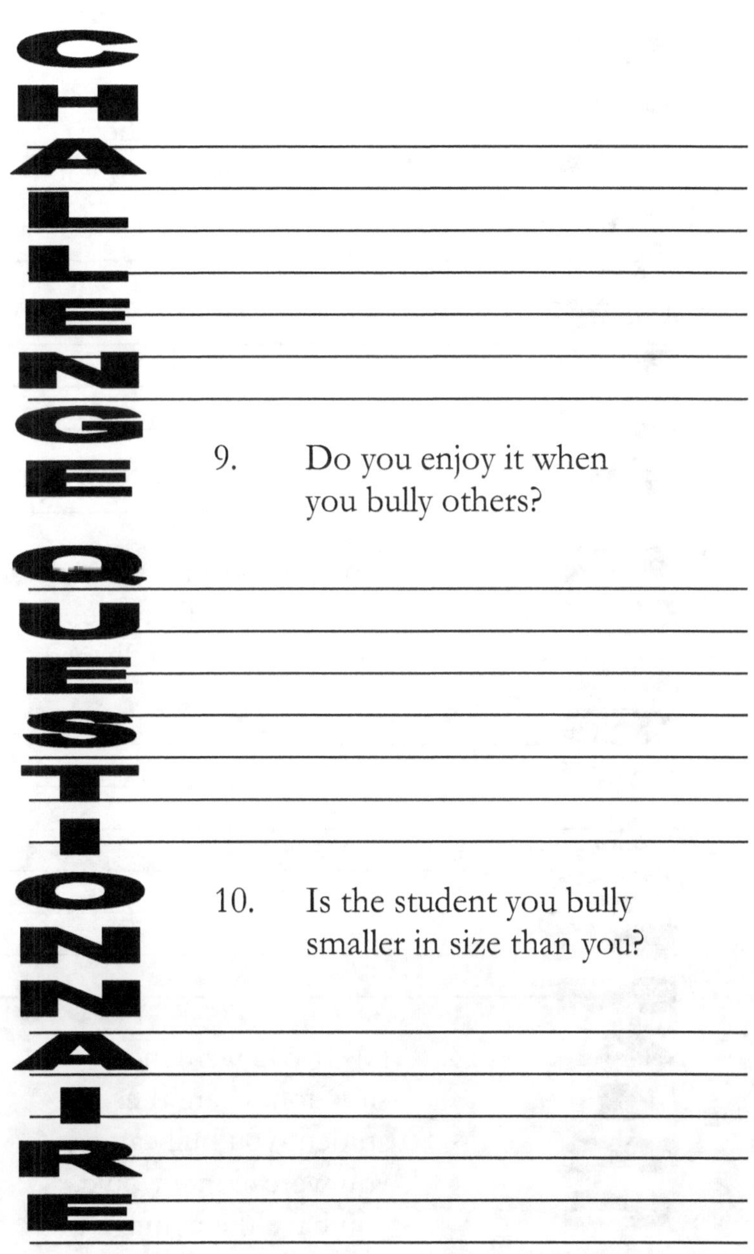

9. Do you enjoy it when you bully others?

10. Is the student you bully smaller in size than you?

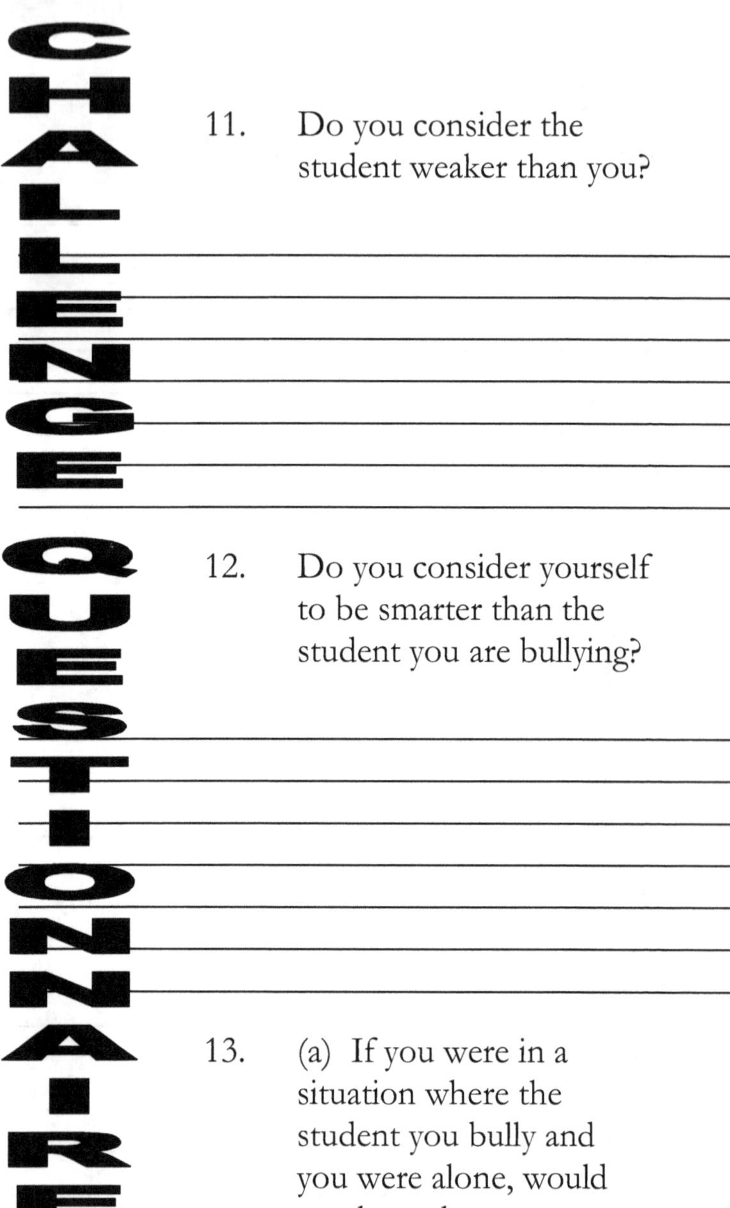

11. Do you consider the student weaker than you?

12. Do you consider yourself to be smarter than the student you are bullying?

13. (a) If you were in a situation where the student you bully and you were alone, would you have the courage to

CHALLENGE QUESTIONNAIRE

bully that person by yourself because you think you could get away with it? (b) Why?

____

14. (a) Do you only bully a student when you are with a group? (b) Are you afraid to bully a student by myself? (c) If so, why?

CHALLENGE QUESTIONNAIRE

15. Do you initiate the bullying?

16. Do you feel safe in a group when you are bullying a student?

17. (a) Do you know that bullying activity taken to an extreme can be considered a crime depending on your age?

CHALLENGE QUESTIONNAIRE

(b) Is bullying someone that's important to you?

18. Are you a spectator, on hand for support and/or actively be involved, when a student is being bullied?

19. As a spectator or watching someone being

CHALLENGE QUESTIONNAIRE

bullied, how does that make you feel?

20. What do you feel in your heart when you are bullying a student?

21. Does it make you feel like you really don't want to do this anymore?

CHALLENGE QUESTIONNAIRE

22. (a) Does it make you feel in control? (b) What is the purpose of you feeling in control in this type of situation?

23. Do you understand that the student you are bullying is smaller in size than you and/or weaker than you?

24. Does it matter to you that people know that bullies mistreat students who are "smaller than you?

25. Does it matter to you that others know that you only pick on those students who are weaker" than you?

CHALLENGE QUESTIONNAIRE

26. Did you know that people who are not bullies think that bullies are cowards because they pick on students who are smaller and/or weaker than they are? Does that matter to you?

27. Does it matter to you that people think that

CHALLENGE QUESTIONNAIRE

you would not have the courage to pick on students larger than you or stronger than you?

28. Have you considered that others think that you pick on students smaller and weaker than you are to draw attention away from yourself?

CHALLENGE QUESTIONNAIRE

29. Did you know that if you admit to yourself that you have hurt feelings will help you not to hurt other students and that this is the first step to feeling better?

30. (a) Did you know that sometimes when we face our hurtful feelings that it makes us cry? (b) Did you know that crying in some instances is not a sign of weakness, but a sign of strength and healing from hurtful feelings and is a release?

CHALLENGE QUESTIONNAIRE

31. How do you feel about crying?

32. (a) Can you reach deep down, for the sake of changing, face your pain in a constructive manner meaning that you will not hurt other students because you are hurting?

CHALLENGE QUESTIONNAIRE

(b) Instead, you will seek ways to be helped from your hurt feelings?

____
____
____
____
____
____
____

33. Do you understand that you are facing your pain because you want it to go away? (b) Are you willing to be strong to face your pain? That takes "real" strength. (c) Are you willing to display this strength?

____
____
____
____
____

34. Sometimes it takes strength to step out and be different. By being different you embark on a new path or journey for your life. Do you want to travel down the new path of changing your course in life simply by changing your attitude? That's how you start.

35. (a) Did you know that you are very intelligent? This is evident because you were willing to take this challenge. You want change and doing things

CHALLENGE QUESTIONNAIRE

differently brings change. Doing the same thing over and over again expecting different results will not bring change, but chaos. How do you feel about that?

36. Are your grades the grades you want to make? You can study harder to achieve the goal of making better grades. There are tutors who can help you. Ask your teacher, school counselor or principal. They will be glad to help guide you. If you need

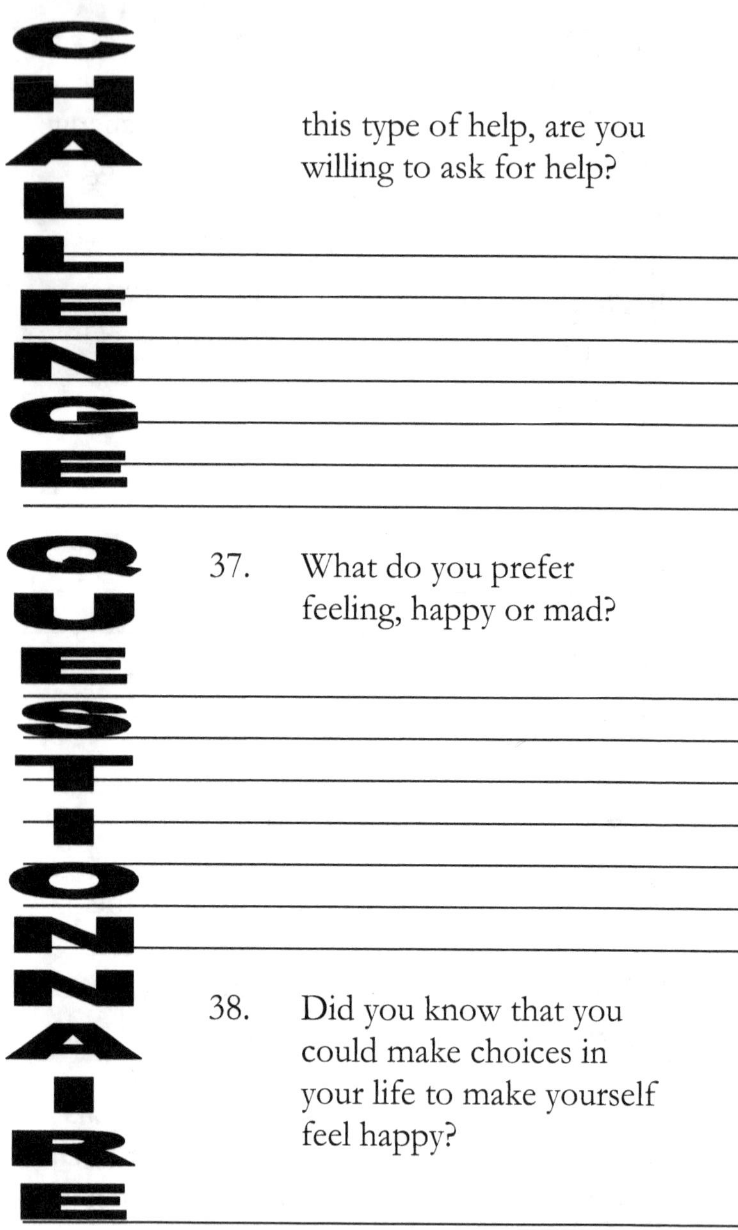

this type of help, are you willing to ask for help?

37. What do you prefer feeling, happy or mad?

38. Did you know that you could make choices in your life to make yourself feel happy?

CHALLENGE QUESTIONNAIRE

39. If you have goals in life to achieve something that will help you and your family, do you believe you can achieve it?

40. Are you willing to go to the library to look in the occupational reference book to see what types of occupations there are in the U.S. in order to see what you might be

CHALLENGE QUESTIONNAIRE

interested in? Search Department of Labor Occupations.

41. Are you willing to go to the library to look up this reference book or search online?

42. Do you feel like you are stuck in life? You're not.

CHALLENGE QUESTIONNAIRE

Time brings about change.

43. Feeling stuck is like being in a box. Do you know that you can think outside-the-box right now?

44. Do you know that thinking outside the box (*i.e.*, thinking about things

CHALLENGE QUESTIONNAIRE

that you would like to achieve in life, even though you may not have resources in place to do so at this time, will give you a sense of freedom? Take the time right now to think of something as if you have all the financial resources right now to do it. How does that make you feel?

45. Do you want to change how you treat other students?

CHALLENGE QUESTIONNAIRE

46. If you decide to change, would you be willing to help others think positively?

47. Would you be willing to become a role model of positive change?

CHALLENGE QUESTIONNAIRE

48. Would you be willing to ask for forgiveness from the students you bullied and mean it? That would be huge!

49. Are you ready to begin the first day of the rest of your life? Then start thinking differently how you treat other students. You learned about "S.E.A." Sympathy, Empathy and Apathy. Going forward you will want to practice sympathy and empathy.

CHALLENGE QUESTIONAIRE

50. Write an essay about what you want to do differently with your life that could be a positive impact on the lives of others. You may include ideas that could positively affect people globally. You have a lot of good things in you. Let it come out. Start thinking about it and believe in yourself. It is possible.

CHALLENGE QUESTIONNAIRE

CHALLENGE QUESTIONNAIRE

CHALLENGE QUESTIONNAIRE

Thank you for reading this book and for taking the Challenge Questionnaire to encourage you to become a positive role model.

Welcome to the first day of the rest of your life!

www.ingramcontent.com/pod-product-compliance
Lightning Source LLC
LaVergne TN
LVHW010118170826
845678LV00012B/2470

* 9 7 8 0 5 7 8 6 2 6 7 8 9 *